Through the Mind's Window

Discover the Art of Seeing Life Beyond Your Thoughts

Through the Mind's Window!

ISBN (**978-93-344-0284-1**).

First Edition, 2025

Cover Design by [REMI]

Edited by [REMI]

Disclaimer: This book is intended to provide inspiration and guidance. It is not a substitute for professional advice, diagnosis, or treatment. Readers should seek the advice of qualified professionals for any personal concerns. The author and publisher disclaim

Published by Remi Palapu

CONTENTS

Introduction

There is a constant murmur within us.

A restless voice that never sleeps.
It comments, it criticizes, it imagines, it remembers. It creates a thousand worlds every hour, pulling us in and out of joy, sorrow, fear, and hope.

Most of us live entirely inside this voice, believing it to be who we are.
But what if you are not the voice?
What if you are the listener?

To watch your thoughts from a distance is like stepping out of a storm and suddenly noticing the sky above it. You are no longer being blown away by the winds of the mind—you are standing on the shore, observing the waves.

This book is an invitation to shift from identification to observation. To discover the quiet presence that is always there, just behind the noise. When you begin to see your thoughts from a 3rd-person perspective, something remarkable happens:

- You realize thoughts are visitors, not masters.
- You feel emotions without being consumed by them.
- You find space in moments that once felt suffocating.
- You awaken to a freedom that is simple, yet profound.

This is not about rejecting the mind. It is about befriending it—like watching a child play, sometimes messy, sometimes brilliant, but always innocent in its own way.

The chapters ahead will take you on a journey—first into the storm of thought, then into the discovery of the witness, and finally into living as that silent presence in everyday life. Each chapter will offer reflections, stories, and gentle practices so that you not only read about awareness, but taste it, here and now.

To witness your mind is to meet yourself. Not the self-shaped by memory, opinion, or fear, but the deeper self—the one that simply *is*.

Let us begin this journey together, not by changing who you are, but by remembering who you have always been: **the silent observer, the witness within.**

Prologue – The Watcher's Whisper

Close your eyes for a moment.
Notice the tide within you.

A thought rises. Another follows.
Memories, plans, fragments of voices—
like clouds drifting, like waves unfolding.

Do you see?
You are not the cloud.
You are not the wave.
You are the sky that holds them,
the ocean that allows them to pass.

There is a presence within you,
silent, unhurried, untouched.
It watches without judgment.
It listens without becoming.
It waits without seeking.

This presence has always been here.
When you were a child,
when you dreamed of tomorrow,
when you worried about yesterday—
it was here, silently observing.

This book is not about becoming someone new.
It is about remembering the one who has never left—
the witness, the watcher,
the quiet flame behind your thoughts.

Take a breath.
Take another.
Step gently into the pages ahead.
The journey begins not in words,
but in the silent space from which they arise.

Acknowledgments

This book is not mine alone. It is a reflection of countless moments, voices, and unseen hands that have guided me toward this path of awareness.

To the quiet breath that reminded me to pause,
to the restless thoughts that taught me patience,
to silence, which whispered wisdom when words could not—
I bow in gratitude.

To the teachers hidden in every joy and every struggle,
to the fleeting moments that opened into eternity,
to the mysteries that revealed themselves only

in stillness—

I offer my thanks.

To every reader holding this book: may these pages not instruct, but invite; not dictate, but awaken. May you discover, within your own gaze, the vastness that waits beyond thought.

And above all, to Life itself—the eternal storyteller—thank you for allowing me to glimpse, if only for a moment, the beauty seen through the mind's window.

Dedication

To the silent witness within us all—

the one who watches without judgment,

who waits with infinite patience,

who sees life not through the noise of thought,

but through the quiet window of awareness.

This book is for you.

Chapter 1 – The Observer and the Observed

There is a moment—silent, subtle, almost invisible—when you realize that you are not just your thoughts.
It happens in the space between a breath and the next heartbeat, when a whisper of awareness opens its eyes inside you.

Have you ever caught yourself *watching* a thought?
Perhaps you were walking under the sky, and suddenly noticed your mind rushing ahead—planning, worrying, replaying scenes like an endless film. In that instant, something curious happened: part of you was swept inside the story, yet another part stood outside, quietly witnessing.

That quiet witness is the **Observer**. The endless chatter is the **Observed**.

One is like the still surface of a lake. The other, like ripples caused by the restless wind.

Most of us spend our lives being tossed about by the ripples, forgetting that we are, in truth, the lake itself—vast, deep, and calm at its heart. But the moment you glimpse the Observer, even for a breath, you feel an untold freedom. The thought may still dance and shout, but now it is not *you*. It is simply something you can watch.

This realization is not cold or distant. It is alive. It is magical. It is the doorway to seeing life differently. Imagine sitting on a hilltop, watching the valley below. The people, the roads, the rushing rivers—none of them disturb your stillness. Your awareness is the hilltop, your thoughts the valley.

The journey of this book begins here—with the discovery that **you are both the watcher and the watched, but your true home is in the watcher.**

And once you learn to rest there, a new world unfolds—one of clarity, stillness, and an intimacy with life so tender that even a falling leaf feels like a revelation.

A Quiet Moment for You

Sit quietly for a few breaths.

Close your eyes.

Notice a thought rising—perhaps about today, tomorrow, or yesterday.

Now gently step back, as if watching a bird fly across the sky.

The thought comes. The thought goes.

But you remain—the sky itself.

Chapter 2 – Thought as a Storyteller

Every thought you have is a story.
Some are brief—like sparks that appear and vanish in an instant.
Some are elaborate—woven tapestries of memory, imagination, hope, and fear.

Your mind, without rest, spins these tales:
'You must achieve this.'
'You should have done that.'
'What if tomorrow goes wrong?'

Have you noticed how convincing these stories feel? As if the mind were a master actor, playing every role—hero, villain, victim, rescuer—while you sit in the audience, forgetting that it's only a performance.

But here is the secret: **you are not the story; you are the one listening to it.**

Thoughts are clever, magical storytellers. They dress themselves in the costumes of truth, yet much of what they whisper is only imagination. One moment they show you a world of success and joy, the next they paint shadows of fear and doubt. And often, without realizing, we believe every word.

But when you pause and listen closely, you may discover something wondrous. The storyteller is tireless, yes—but it is not all of you. You are more than the stage, more than the tale. You are also the silent witness in the background—the reader of the story, not the words on the page.

Imagine holding a book in your hands. As you read, you might cry, laugh, or tremble. Yet part of you knows—you are not *inside* the book. You are holding it. In the same way, every thought is just a storybook moment. Some inspire, some wound, some heal—but none can touch the vastness of who you truly are.

The mind will always weave its stories. That is its nature. The gift is not in silencing it forever, but in realizing you can step back, smile, and say:

'Ah, another tale... thank you, but I don't have to believe every chapter.'

A Quiet Moment for You

Take a notebook.

Write down one thought that repeats often in your mind.

Now, re-read it as if it were a line from a novel—not your life, just a character speaking.

Ask yourself: *Would I believe this if it were just a story?*

Feel the lightness when you remember—you are not trapped in the book; you are the reader.

Chapter 3 – The Art of Gentle Detachment

There is a way of looking at your thoughts without clinging to them.
Not rejecting. Not fighting. Not drowning in them.
Simply watching—like clouds drifting across an endless sky.

This is the art of gentle detachment.

When a thought arises—

'I am not good enough'

'What if I fail'

'They should have treated me better'—instead of wrestling with it, imagine opening your hand and letting it rest there, lightly. You don't grip it. You don't push it away. You simply hold it softly, as though it were a feather carried by the wind.

Gentle detachment is not coldness, nor indifference.
It is spaciousness.
It is a kindness that allows every thought to appear and pass, without giving it the power to command your soul.

Think of the ocean. Waves rise and fall endlessly. Some are calm, some are fierce. Yet the ocean never clings to one wave. It allows each to come, each to go. In the same way, you too can allow thoughts to rise and fall, while resting in the vastness beneath them.

This art is gentle because it does not demand perfection. You do not need to force the mind into silence. You only need to step back, breathe, and remember: *I am not the thought. I am the space in which the thought appears.*

And slowly, something miraculous happens. The grip loosens. The storm softens. You begin to sense a freedom that was always waiting, just beyond the noise.

A Quiet Moment for You

The next time a troubling thought arises,

pause.

Take a slow breath.

Say softly within: *I see you. You may stay, you may leave—I will not cling.*

Notice how the thought, without resistance or fuel, begins to drift on its own.

Chapter 4 – Befriending the Inner Voice

There is a voice that never stops speaking.
Sometimes it whispers, sometimes it shouts, sometimes it echoes like a song on repeat.
It tells you stories of yesterday, it paints fears of tomorrow, it comments on everything you do.

This is the inner voice.

For most of us, it feels like a constant companion—though not always a kind one.
It judges. It doubts. It compares. It reminds you of wounds long past.
Yet if you pause and listen closely, you may discover: this voice is not your enemy.

It is, in truth, a messenger.
It speaks in the language it has learned—from

childhood, from society, from memory.
It tries to protect, to warn, to prepare.
But often, it knows only fear.

To befriend the inner voice is not to obey its every word.
It is to meet it with compassion, as you would a child who is frightened.
When it says, *'You're not enough,'* you don't have to believe it—
but you may softly respond, *'I hear you, and I choose differently.'*

The moment you stop wrestling with this voice and instead meet it with kindness, something shifts.
The sharp edges soften.
The noise becomes less commanding.
The voice, once a tyrant, begins to transform into a guide.

And here lies the secret: when befriended, the inner voice can learn a new song—
one of encouragement, of gentleness, of wisdom.

You do not silence it by force.
You heal it through love.

A Quiet Moment for You

The next time your inner voice criticizes you, pause.

Instead of pushing it away, place your hand over your heart and say:

'Thank you for speaking. I choose to see myself with kindness.'

Notice how the voice begins to soften when it is no longer met with resistance.

Chapter 5 – The Power of Pause

Life rushes.

Thoughts tumble.

Moments blur into one another until you are no longer living them—you are chasing them.

And yet, hidden in plain sight, lies a secret doorway: **the pause.**

To pause is to step out of the storm for a breath.

It is the still point between inhale and exhale, where time itself bows in silence. It is the gentle reminder that you are not a machine of endless doing—you are a being, meant also for stillness.

Think of a musician. Without the pause, music would be noise.

Think of a painter. Without empty space, colors

would lose their meaning.

Think of a sentence. Without a comma, words would collide.

In the same way, without pause, life loses its depth.

The power of pause is not about withdrawal from life—it is about presence *within* life. When you pause, you are not escaping. You are arriving.

Imagine standing at the edge of a forest. If you rush, all you see are shapes and shadows. But if you pause, you begin to notice—the curve of each leaf, the breath of the wind, the birdsong hidden in silence.

The world does not reveal its treasures to those who hurry.

It opens to those who linger.

A pause can be as small as a single breath.
It can be a moment of closing your eyes before you speak.
It can be waiting before you react, letting the waters of emotion settle so clarity may rise.

The pause is not weakness.
It is power—the kind of power that does not shout but steadies.
It allows wisdom to walk in, where impulse once ruled.

In the pause, you discover space between you and your thoughts.
You realize you are not bound to every storm they bring.
You can watch them pass, just as clouds drift across a sky that never loses its stillness.

The more you honor the pause, the more life begins to breathe with you.

Stress softens.

Clarity deepens.

Joy sneaks back in.

And slowly, you realize: the pause was never an interruption to life—

it was the doorway back to it.

A Quiet Moment for You

The next time you feel hurried or restless, stop for just three breaths.

Let the first breath slow your body.

Let the second calm your mind.

Let the third open your heart.

Ask yourself gently: *'Am I living, or am I rushing past life?'*

Step back into the moment, and let the pause carry you home.

Chapter 6 – Shadows and Light of the Mind

Within the landscape of your mind, there are valleys of shadow and mountains bathed in light. Both belong to you. Both shape the way you see the world.

The shadows hold your doubts, fears, regrets, and the echoes of wounds you thought you had forgotten. They whisper of past mistakes and uncertain futures. Sometimes they appear larger than life, stretching across your path like giants.

And yet—without shadow, would you recognize light?

Light reveals your hopes, your clarity, your joy. It is the quiet strength that rises when you least expect it, the warmth that reminds you of your true nature. The mind is never just one or the other—it is a dance, a shifting sky where clouds and sunlight share the same horizon.

But here is the secret: you are neither the shadow nor the light. You are the sky itself, vast enough to hold them both.

The mistake we often make is identifying with only one side. We cling to the light and resist the shadow, or we sink into the shadow and forget the light is still shining somewhere within us. True awareness is the art of seeing both with compassion, without running from either.

A shadow is not your enemy. It is a messenger. Fear may be showing you where courage longs to grow. Pain may be pointing you toward healing. Doubt may be urging you to look deeper for truth. If you pause and listen, the shadow often carries the seed of transformation.

And the light? The light reminds you that no shadow is permanent. Just as dawn always follows the darkest night, so too does clarity return after confusion. Light is the invitation back to trust, back to openness, back to love.

Imagine sitting in a room with a single candle. The flame glows, and shadows stretch across the walls. Do you curse the shadows, or do you marvel that such a small flame can hold back the darkness? Both exist in the same space—and both teach you something profound.

So, when you feel overwhelmed by the shadows of your mind, remember: you are the one who holds the candle. You are the witness who sees them flicker. And when the light feels too fleeting, know that it does not need to be eternal to be real. Even the smallest spark can guide you forward.

Life is not about erasing shadows or chasing endless light. It is about embracing the whole sky within you—the storms, the sunlight, and the calm that cradles them both.

Because when you can hold shadow and light in the same breath, you step into the vastness of who you truly are.

A Quiet Moment for You

Close your eyes and take a slow breath. Picture your mind as a wide sky.

Notice the light—the moments of gratitude, love, or peace that glow within you.

Then notice the shadow—your fears, doubts, or unspoken worries.

Instead of pushing one away, let them both exist. Whisper inwardly:

'I am the sky. I can hold it all.'

Chapter 7 – Listening to Life's Whispers

Life is always speaking.
Not in the noise of traffic, nor in the endless chatter of the mind—but in whispers so soft that only a still heart can hear them.

These whispers come when you least expect them—while watching the rain slide down a window, when the wind brushes gently against your face, in the hush between two breaths. They are subtle, delicate threads of guidance woven into the fabric of your everyday moments.

But most of the time, they are drowned out. We run too fast, think too loud, want too much. The whispers are not absent—we have simply forgotten how to listen.

Imagine a friend trying to share a secret with you in a crowded room. If you lean in close, if you hush your mind, you can hear the words that no one else can. Life is that friend. Always leaning in, always waiting, and always whispering.

The whispers may appear as intuition—a sudden knowing that you cannot explain, a nudge toward a choice, or a gentle resistance when something is not right. They may come as wonder—the way a sunset stops you mid-step, or how a child's laughter reminds you of innocence you thought was lost. They may come as silence—the kind that holds you without words, showing you that peace does not need to be earned.

The art of listening to life's whispers is not about effort. It is about softening. Slowing down. Becoming empty enough so that what is subtle can enter.

Ask yourself: When was the last time I truly listened—not just with my ears, but with my whole being?
To a bird singing at dawn.
To the rhythm of my own heartbeat.
To the spaces between words in a conversation.

When you listen deeply, you begin to realize something extraordinary: life has always been guiding you. Not through force, but through whispers. Not through command, but through invitation.

Every whisper carries a secret message: *'You are not lost. You are part of something vast and tender. Trust the rhythm. Trust the silence. Trust that you are being carried.'*

So, listen. Listen not for answers, but for presence. Listen not to control, but to surrender.

Because when you learn to hear life's whispers, you no longer walk alone. You walk with the universe at your side.

A Quiet Moment for You

Sit quietly for a few moments today. Close your eyes, breathe gently, and ask life to whisper to you. Don't strain. Don't expect. Just listen. It may come as a feeling, an image, a word, or pure silence. Accept whatever arrives.

Whisper back: *'I am here. I am listening.'*

Chapter 8 – Beyond the Storm of Thoughts

Thoughts come like storms.
Dark, restless clouds gather inside the mind—swirling with memories, fears, plans, and worries. Sometimes they arrive suddenly, sometimes they build slowly until you find yourself caught in a downpour of inner noise.

When you are inside the storm, it feels endless. Every thought flashes like lightning, every doubt rumbles like thunder. You try to outrun them, but the harder you resist, the more powerful they become.

But here is a secret: *you are not the storm.* You are the sky that holds it. The storm may roar, the winds may whip, but the sky is untouched. Always vast. Always clear behind the clouds.

This is the essence of freedom—seeing thoughts for what they are: movements in the mind, not the essence of who you are. A thought may say *'you are not enough'*, but notice—it is only a sound in your head, not the truth of your being. Another may say *'what if everything goes wrong'*, yet it dissolves as quickly as it came.

When you step back, when you rest as the observer, you begin to see: thoughts are visitors. They come and go, but they do not define you.

And something miraculous happens when you stop chasing or fighting the storm. Slowly, the clouds begin to thin. A patch of blue appears. Light filters through. The storm passes—not because you controlled it, but because you allowed it.

In this clarity beyond the storm, you feel a deep stillness. A peace untouched by thought. And from this space, wisdom flows—not as noise, but as knowing.

Remember this: storms will come again. That is their nature. But you no longer have to fear them. You have discovered the vastness beyond them.

Every time a storm rises, smile gently and say: *'This too will pass. I am the sky, not the storm.'*

A Quiet Moment for You

The next time you feel overwhelmed by racing thoughts, pause. Close your eyes and imagine yourself as the vast sky. See the thoughts as clouds passing through. Some may be heavy and dark, others light and fleeting. Watch them without clinging, without judgment. Let them drift.

Feel the quiet spaciousness that remains when you stop identifying with the storm. That is your true self.

Chapter 9 – The Unfolding Silence

After every storm, there is a hush. The world seems to pause—the air feels lighter, the earth sighs, the sky reveals its quiet vastness once more. This is not just the silence of absence, but the silence of presence—alive, breathing, infinite.

The same happens within us. When thoughts settle, when the inner storm dissolves, something gentle begins to unfold. It is not forced, not created by effort. It simply reveals itself, like dawn rising over a dark horizon.

This silence is not empty. It is full—full of clarity, full of awareness, full of life. In its embrace, worries lose their grip, questions soften, and the restless mind bows to something greater.

Have you ever listened closely, not to words, but to the space between them? Not to the sound of music, but the stillness in which music appears? That stillness is always there, quietly holding everything.

The unfolding silence within you is that same space.
It does not judge.
It does not rush.
It simply *is*.

The more you rest here, the more you realize: you are not separate from it. You *are* this silence. Thoughts are guests, emotions are waves, but silence is the ocean that holds them all.

And here lies a profound gift—when you live from silence, life itself becomes lighter. Decisions feel clearer. Relationships grow gentler. Even challenges lose their sharpness, because silence softens their edges.

Silence does not mean withdrawing from life. On the contrary, it allows you to enter life more fully, more authentically. It teaches you that you don't need to shout to be heard, nor hurry to arrive. You are already complete, already whole, in this quiet unfolding.

So breathe deeply, and let the silence open inside you. Like a flower opening its petals to the morning sun, allow your being to open to the calm, luminous presence that was always there.

A Quiet Moment for You

Find a moment in your day where you sit quietly, without distractions. Close your eyes and take three deep breaths. Then, instead of focusing on thoughts or sounds, notice the silence beneath them. The more you listen, the more it expands.

Stay with it for a few minutes. Let the silence speak to you—not with words, but with presence.

Chapter 10 – The Window Becomes a Door

At first, awareness feels like peeking through a window.
You stand inside, looking out—observing thoughts, emotions, and the rhythm of life. The glass is clear, and for the first time, you realize you are not trapped in the storm—you are watching it.

But something miraculous happens when you linger at this window long enough: it begins to dissolve. What was once a boundary becomes an opening. The window turns into a door.

A door to what?
To life itself. To a deeper, freer way of being.

You are no longer the one merely watching thoughts—you are the one walking beyond them. Stepping through this doorway means stepping into a space where the mind no longer controls the script, where stories lose their power, and where the vastness of your true self welcomes you home.

Through the door, you do not escape life—you enter it more fully. The laughter feels richer, the silence more profound. Even pain, when it comes, is no longer a prison—it is a passing guest.

The door does not open with force. It opens with surrender.
It does not require effort, only willingness—to trust, to release, to walk gently into the unknown.

Once you step through, you realize the window was never really there. The door was always open. You were always free. It was only the fog of thought that made you believe you were confined.

And now, with each breath, each pause, each moment of awareness, the doorway widens. You no longer peer at life from a distance—you *merge* with it. You taste the sky, you feel the ground, you dissolve into the music of existence.

The window has become a door, and the door has become the path back to yourself.

A Quiet Moment for You

The next time you catch yourself observing your thoughts, imagine a window before you. Watch gently, without judgment. Then, with your breath, visualize the window softening, melting away into an open doorway.

Ask yourself: *What would it feel like to step beyond this thought, into freedom?*

Even for a moment, allow yourself to walk through that invisible door into the living presence of now.

Chapter 11 – Distancing Without Escaping

There is a delicate art in watching the mind without running from it.
Too often, when thoughts trouble us, we want to escape—into distraction, into busyness, into denial. But true freedom is not found in fleeing. It is found in *distancing without escaping.*

Imagine standing by a river. Thoughts rush like water, carrying sticks, leaves, sometimes storms. You do not need to dam the river. You do not need to dive in. You simply step back and watch the current flow.

This step back is not avoidance—it is awareness. It gives you space. Space to breathe. Space to remember: *I am not the water. I am the sky above it.*

Distancing without escaping means holding life with gentle hands. You do not reject the thought, nor do you cling to it. You see it for what it is: a passing formation, no more permanent than a cloud drifting through the sky.

The power of this practice lies in its subtlety. Escape still keeps the thought alive—it hides in the shadows, waiting. But when you create distance with awareness, the thought dissolves naturally, like mist under the morning sun.

This is the freedom of the observer:
to be close enough to witness,
yet spacious enough not to be consumed.

You begin to realize that problems lose their grip when you stop wrestling with them. A memory becomes just a flicker. A worry becomes just a ripple. Even fear, when observed with presence, softens into nothingness.

You are not escaping life—you are stepping deeper into it. With clarity. With openness. With the courage to see and yet remain free.

A Quiet Moment for You

When a troubling thought arises today, resist the urge to push it away. Instead, pause. Take one slow, deep breath. Then silently say: *'I see you, but I am not you.'*

Notice the gentle distance it creates. You are no longer caught. You are watching from the shore.

Chapter 12 – Breathing Space for the Mind

The mind, like a crowded marketplace, is often filled with voices, footsteps, and restless movement. Thoughts jostle one another for attention. Worries shout, memories whisper, plans march ahead with urgency. It is no wonder we feel suffocated.

But just as a marketplace has an open sky above it, so too does your mind have a vastness beyond the chatter. All it needs is space.

Breath is the doorway to that space. With one conscious inhale, you pause the noise. With one gentle exhale, you release its grip. The breath does not silence the marketplace—it simply lifts you above it, into the spaciousness where thoughts no longer crowd you.

This breathing space is not about controlling thoughts or pushing them away. It is about creating room. A single pause. A single inhale that says, *'I belong to this moment, not to the storm of my mind.'*

In that pause, clarity arises. You begin to see thoughts not as commands, but as suggestions. Not as truth, but as passing breezes. The mind softens, like dust settling after the wind has stilled.

The beauty is that this breathing space is always available. You don't have to travel to a mountain or seek silence in a cave. It is here—in the air filling your lungs, in the rhythm of your heart, in the stillness between one thought and the next.

When the mind feels tight, knotted, or crowded, invite a breath to untangle it. Let your inhale expand like the sky, and your exhale carry away the clutter. Soon, you will feel the space open—not outside you, but within you.

For the truth is simple:
a spacious mind is a peaceful mind.
And a peaceful mind is a window to life itself.

A Quiet Moment for You

Pause now. Close your eyes. Take three slow breaths, each deeper than the one before. As you inhale, imagine your mind expanding like a clear sky. As you exhale, release the noise like leaves falling away.

Stay here for a few moments. Notice how the space within you feels wider than the thoughts passing through.

Chapter 13 – The Unfolding Silence

Silence is not the absence of sound. It is the presence of something deeper—an alive stillness that patiently waits beneath the layers of noise.

Often, we fear silence. We fill it with chatter, distractions, and endless doing. But silence is not empty. It is full—full of clarity, full of presence, full of truths that words can never quite touch.

When you rest in silence, thoughts lose their urgency. They may still arise, but they are no longer commanders. They are simply visitors. And you—the host—stand spacious, calm, and unmoved.

Silence does not arrive with force. It unfolds, like dawn breaking across the horizon. It softens the edges of your mind. It eases the tightness in your chest. It invites you to listen, not with your ears, but with your whole being.

In this unfolding silence, something magical happens: you begin to hear life itself. The rustle of leaves is no longer just sound; it is wisdom. The stillness between your heartbeats is no longer just pause; it is eternity. Even the breath becomes a song, reminding you that existence is simple, steady, and miraculous.

Silence is not something you create. It is something you uncover—like brushing sand off a buried jewel. It is already here, beneath the thoughts, beneath the noise, beneath the restless searching.

To sit in silence is to sit in the lap of life. It is to rediscover that you are not separate from the flow—you *are* the flow. And the flow has always been silent.

So, when silence unfolds within you, do not rush to fill it. Stay. Rest. Breathe. Let it stretch its wings. And slowly, gently, you will see: the silence was never empty. It was always you.

A Quiet Moment for You

Find a quiet corner. Sit with your back straight and eyes gently closed. Take a deep breath in, and exhale slowly. For the next three minutes, do nothing—just notice. Notice the faint sounds around you, notice the space between them, and then notice the silence underneath everything.

Ask yourself: *What is this silence trying to show me?*

Do not look for an answer. Simply listen.

Chapter 14 – The Voice That Never Stops

There is a voice inside your head that never seems to rest. It comments, it narrates, it compares, it judges. From the moment you wake until the final seconds before sleep, it keeps spinning its stories, as if silence were dangerous and words were survival.

This voice is not you, though it often pretends to be. It borrows your memories, wears your fears, echoes your desires, and whispers your doubts. Sometimes it plays the role of friend, sometimes enemy, but always—always—it speaks.

Have you noticed how it interrupts even the simplest moment? You watch a sunset, and the voice says, *'How beautiful, I should capture this.'*

You hear laughter, and the voice wonders, *'What do they think of me?'* Even in joy, it seeks control; even in sorrow, it demands attention.

And yet, this voice is not the problem. The problem is our blind loyalty to it. We believe its every story, as if it were a sacred truth. But when you begin to watch the voice instead of following it, something shifts.

The chatter no longer defines you. It becomes like the sound of rain on the roof—constant, sometimes heavy, sometimes light, but no longer personal. You are not trapped in it. You are the one listening.

This recognition is liberation. Because once you know the voice is not you, you begin to smile at it. When it worries, you breathe. When it doubts, you stay still. When it shouts, you listen gently, the way you would to a child who is afraid.

And slowly, the voice loses its power. It still speaks, but it no longer rules. It becomes background music, while the real melody of life—the quiet joy of being—takes the stage.

The voice may never stop. But your identification with it can. And in that space, you find freedom—not from thoughts, but from being possessed by them.

A Quiet Moment for You

Today, notice your inner voice as if it were a character in a play. Whenever it speaks, ask gently:

'Is this truth, or just a story?'

Do not fight the voice. Simply watch. Smile at its persistence. And then—return to your breath, your body, your presence. The voice may continue, but you will no longer be its captive.

Chapter 15 – You Are Not the Thought

A thought arrives.

It could be gentle as a feather—*'I hope they like me.'*

Or sharp as a blade—*'I will never be enough.'*

It could sparkle with promise—*'Tomorrow will be better.'*

Or weigh heavy like a stone—*'I am failing.'*

The thought appears, lingers, and fades.

And yet, how quickly we make it our identity.

We say, *'I am anxious,'* not *'An anxious thought is passing through.'*

We say, *'I am angry,'* not *'A wave of anger has touched me.'*

But here lies the secret:

You are not the thought.

You are the vast sky through which thoughts move.
The bird is not the sky; the cloud is not the sky.
And you are not the thought.

When you believe every thought, you shrink to its size. If the thought is heavy, you feel heavy. If the thought is dark, your world seems dark. But when you step back—when you see the thought for what it is, just a flicker of energy, a visitor—you expand again.

The truth is: you have thoughts, but you are not the thinker. Thoughts arise, but they do not define you. They are passing weather, while you are the infinite space in which they appear.

Imagine standing at the edge of the ocean, watching waves rise and fall. Do you claim each wave as yourself? Or do you simply watch, knowing the ocean is greater than the wave?

So too with thoughts. Watch them. Let them pass. Smile at their drama. Do not hold them too tightly, for they are not you.

The moment you see this, even for a breath, something shifts. The grip loosens. A freedom enters. Life becomes lighter, because you no longer carry every passing story as your identity.

You are not the thought.
You are the witness of the thought.
And in that realization lies peace.

A Quiet Moment for You

Whenever a strong thought arises today, place your hand gently on your heart and whisper to yourself:
'This is a thought. It is not me.'

Breathe deeply. Watch how the thought softens, like mist dissolving in the morning sun.

Chapter 16 – Shadows of the Past, Echoes of the Future

The mind is a restless traveller.
Rarely does it sit in the quiet of now.

It wanders backward—
to moments wrapped in regret,
to memories tinged with loss,
to victories that once made the heart swell.
It gathers them all and whispers:
'This is who you are.'

Then, without rest, it leaps forward—
into the future's fog,
dreaming, fearing, preparing, imagining.
It creates a thousand possible tomorrows and
asks:
'What if?'

And so, life is lived less in reality
and more in the shadows of the past,
the echoes of the future.

But pause.
Right now, as you read these words,
what is missing?
Not the past. Not the future.
Only this breath. Only this moment.

The past is a ghost—it no longer breathes.
The future is an unborn child—it has not arrived.
But the present...
the present is alive, pulsing, radiant.

When we cling to past shadows,
we carry wounds that no longer bleed.
When we chase future echoes,
we fear storms that may never come.
In both, we lose the gift of here.

The secret is not to erase past or future.
Memories will come, plans will arise.
But to see them as what they are—
reflections in the mind's mirror.
You are not the reflection.
You are the mirror.

Step into the living present,
and both shadows and echoes fall silent.
There, in the stillness of now,
you meet life unfiltered, unbound.

The past cannot chain you.
The future cannot frighten you.
Only this breath, only this moment—
this is your home.

A Quiet Moment for You

When you find yourself lost in past or future today, pause.
Gently name it: *'This is memory.'* or *'This is imagination.'*
Then bring your awareness to your breath.
Feel it rise, feel it fall.
This is the bridge back to the present—your only true place of living.

Chapter 17 – Chaos and Stillness

Life often feels like a storm.

Thoughts rush like wild winds,

emotions roar like thunder,

fears flash like lightning across the inner sky.

In those moments, you may believe

that chaos is all there is—

that the storm will never end.

But pause...

beneath every storm,

there lies a still, unmoving ocean.

The winds may howl, the surface may rage,

yet in the depths, silence abides.

Your mind is the same.

Chaos dances on the surface—

to-do lists, worries, desires, regrets.

But deep within,

there is a stillness untouched,

a sanctuary that no storm can disturb.

The secret is not to fight the chaos,

not to resist the storm.

For resistance only feeds its power.

Instead, step back. Watch. Witness.

See the storm as passing weather.

And when you no longer identify with the whirlwind,

you begin to sink beneath it,

into the calm that is always there.

Stillness is not something you create.

It is what remains when you stop clinging to chaos.

Notice:

even in the loudest noise,

there is a space of silence surrounding it.

Even in the rush of thought,

there is a gap between one thought and the
next.
This gap—this silence—
is your true refuge.

Chaos will always visit.
Stillness will always remain.
Both are part of the dance,
but one is fleeting,
and the other eternal.

When you learn to rest in the stillness,
the chaos loses its power.
It comes, it goes—
like passing clouds in an infinite sky.

And you?
You are the sky.

Quiet Moment for You

Close your eyes for a moment.
Picture your thoughts as waves on the surface of an ocean.
Now, with each breath, imagine yourself sinking deeper—
beneath the noise, beneath the movement—
into the quiet depths where nothing stirs.
Stay there for a few breaths.
This is your stillness. Carry it with you.

Chapter 18 – Stepping Aside

There is a simple secret to peace.
Not conquering thoughts,
not silencing them by force,
not wrestling the mind into submission.

The secret is this:
step aside.

When a river rushes in full flow,
would you stand in its path and fight the current?
Or would you simply step to the bank,
watching the water pass,
untouched, unpulled, unharmed?

The mind too is a river.
It carries stories, judgments, memories,
dreams of tomorrow, shadows of yesterday.
When you stand in its middle,

you get swept away—
tangled in branches, lost in currents,
believing you are the river itself.

But the moment you step aside,
you see.
The thoughts keep flowing,
but you are no longer drowning.
You are the watcher on the bank.
You are free.

This stepping aside is not escape.
It is not denial.
It is clarity.
For when you are no longer caught in the current,
you begin to notice the ripples,
the way the light dances on the surface,
the silence of the forest beyond the water.

And slowly, you realize:
you are not the river.
You are the vastness
in which the river flows.

Step aside,
and life opens into space.
Step aside,
and the mind loses its grip.
Step aside,
and freedom greets you
like an old forgotten friend.

A Quiet Moment for You

Next time a thought troubles you,

do not chase it, do not resist it.

Instead, imagine placing it gently in a river.

See it drift, carried by the flow.

Watch as it disappears around the bend.

You are not the thought—

you are the one who watches it pass.

Chapter 19 – Emotions in the Open Sky

Emotions are clouds.

Some arrive soft and tender,

like morning mist—

a quiet sadness,

a gentle longing.

Others roar in thunder,

dark and heavy,

pouring their storms of anger, fear, or despair.

But no matter how thick the clouds,

the sky remains untouched.

The storm never stains the sky.

It only passes through.

We forget this.

We think we *are* the cloud,

that the sadness is us,

that the anger defines us,

that the storm will never end.

But the truth is vast and luminous:

you are not the cloud.

You are the sky.

Emotions belong to the sky,

but they do not limit it.

They are guests passing through,

not owners of the house.

So let your emotions move.

Let them weep, let them burn, let them dance.

Do not cage them,

do not chase them away.

Simply open the door of awareness,

and watch as they come,

and just as surely—

watch as they go.

The sky does not panic
when the storm arrives.
It knows the storm belongs,
and it knows the storm will leave.

This is freedom:
to feel without becoming.
To allow without clinging.
To welcome the rain,
and to let the sun return,
both held in the same vastness.

You are not your emotions.
You are the infinite sky
in which they rise and fall.

A Quiet Moment for You

When a strong emotion arises,
pause.
Close your eyes and imagine the sky within
you.
See the emotion as a cloud drifting there.
Breathe, and let the cloud move freely.
Notice—it never defines the sky.
And slowly,
you will rest in the vastness that you are.

Chapter 20 – The Third Eye of Awareness

There is an eye that does not belong to the body.
It does not blink,
does not strain,
does not grow weary.

It is not the eye of flesh,
but the eye of truth—
the quiet watcher at the center of your being.

Some call it the **Third Eye**,
some call it intuition,
some call it pure awareness.

Whatever the name,
it is the place within you
that sees without judgment,

that knows without thinking,

that perceives without effort.

When you look through this inner eye,

life changes.

You stop being entangled in the colors and shapes of thought.

You see thoughts themselves

as ripples on the surface of a vast ocean.

Through the Third Eye,

anger is not an enemy,

it is simply energy.

Fear is not a cage,

it is a passing shadow.

Joy is not a possession,

it is a song moving through you.

This eye does not cling to form.

It sees the formless.

It sees what lies behind appearances—

the space, the silence,

the eternal witness.

It is like standing at the top of a mountain.

From there, you see the valleys and rivers,

the storms and sunlight,

the villages and cities—

all of it part of a grand tapestry.

And suddenly,

you realize you are not trapped in one moment,

in one thought,

in one emotion.

You are the seer.

You are the mountain.

The Third Eye opens when you stop trying to control what you see.

It opens when you soften,

when you surrender,

when you allow life to show itself

without resistance.

This is not an achievement.

It is a remembrance.

You are remembering the vast eye of

consciousness

that has always been watching,

always been here.

A Quiet Moment for You

Close your eyes gently.
Bring your awareness to the space between
your eyebrows,
but don't force—just notice.
Breathe slowly.
Now imagine this point is a window,
and through it, you can see thoughts,
emotions,
and even the world itself—
floating by like passing clouds.

Don't interfere.
Just watch.
Feel the stillness of the watcher.
This is the Third Eye opening—
not in mysticism alone,

but in the simple act of resting as pure awareness.

Chapter 21 – Unmasking the Ego

The ego is a clever actor.
It wears masks so skilfully
that you forget it is a mask at all.

One moment it is pride,
declaring, *'I am more.'*
Another moment it is shame,
whispering, *'I am less.'*
It can be a victim,
a hero,
a critic,
a lover,
a rival—
changing costumes faster than your eyes can follow.

But beneath all its disguises,
the ego is only one thing:
a thought that insists it is you.

When you look closely,
you see its tricks.
The ego thrives on comparison,
feeds on approval,
hides in the need to be right,
and trembles at the thought of being nothing.

It is loud,
yet fragile.
It claims ownership of every success
and disowns every failure.
It builds palaces of identity—
but all of sand,
washed away by the next tide of life.

To unmask the ego
is not to destroy it,
but to see it clearly.
When you see the mask,
you are no longer fooled by it.

Notice how the ego reacts to silence—

restless,

uneasy,

trying to fill the stillness with its noise.

Notice how it clings to roles—

parent, worker, seeker,

always saying, *'This is me.'*

But when you step back as the observer,

you smile gently.

Because you know:

the mask is not the face.

The voice is not the truth.

The ego is not you.

When the mask falls,

what remains is simple,

wordless,

free.

The one who observes the ego—

that is your true self.

That is awareness.

That is life, unmasked.

A Quiet Moment for You

The next time you feel offended, praised, or compared—pause.
Instead of reacting, whisper silently to yourself:
'A mask is speaking.'

Notice the space that opens up.
Notice the calm observer behind the mask.
Stay there.
This is freedom—the freedom of seeing without believing the disguise.

Chapter 22 – Freedom from the Inner Judge

There is a voice inside
that carries a gavel.

It sits high in an invisible courtroom,
constantly evaluating,
weighing,
condemning,
rarely forgiving.

This is the inner judge.

It tells you you're not enough.
It tells you, you should have done better.
It digs through your past for evidence
and predicts your future with doubt.
It punishes you for being human,
for being imperfect,
for simply being.

And yet—

who appointed this judge?

Where did it get its authority?

From parents, teachers, society—

voices long past that echo in the mind.

Over time, you believed them so deeply

that you gave them robes and a hammer,

and let them preside over your life.

But the truth is this:

the judge is not real.

It is a habit of thought,

a shadow costume worn by the ego.

Freedom begins the moment you step back

and see the courtroom for what it is—

an empty stage,

with no real jury,

no real verdict,

no real punishment.

When you pause,

when you witness,

the judge stumbles.

Its words lose weight.

Its authority crumbles like dust in the wind.

You realize—

there is no need to silence the judge.

You need only stop obeying it.

You need only see

that the voice is not you.

And in that seeing,

the gavel falls silent.

The courtroom dissolves.

The inner judge vanishes like a dream upon waking.

What remains is mercy.

What remains is tenderness.

What remains is the freedom

to live without standing trial

every moment of your life.

A Quiet Moment for You

Whenever the inner judge rises,
don't fight it.
Instead, whisper softly:
'Thank you, but I don't need a trial today.'

Then breathe into your chest,
feel its rise and fall,
and return to the open sky of awareness.
In this space,
judgment cannot survive.

Chapter 23 – From Doing to Being

For most of your life,
you have been taught to do.

To chase.
To accomplish.
To measure your worth
in tasks completed,
in goals achieved,
in ladders climbed.

Doing became survival.
Doing became identity.
Doing became the rhythm of your days.

But there is another rhythm,
quieter, slower, deeper—
the rhythm of being.

Being does not demand.

It does not rush.

It does not measure.

It simply breathes,

rests,

watches,

exists.

When you shift from doing to being,

life no longer feels like a race.

It becomes a meadow,

where every step is already enough.

The flower does not hurry to bloom.

The river does not struggle to flow.

The bird does not schedule its song.

They are simply themselves—

and in that simplicity,

they are whole.

You too can live this way.

Not abandoning doing,
but letting it rise naturally,
like a wave that comes and goes.
Action born from being is effortless,
graceful,
aligned.
It is no longer a burden,
but an expression of life itself.

When you sit quietly,
without agenda,
without reaching—
you will feel it.
A gentle presence that asks for nothing
and offers everything.

This is the doorway
from striving into serenity,
from effort into ease,
from doing into being.

Here,

life no longer happens *to* you.

It unfolds *through* you.

A Quiet Moment for You

Today, take five minutes to stop doing.

No phone.

No tasks.

No list.

Just sit.

Just breathe.

Just be.

Notice the stillness.

Notice the space.

Notice that even without effort,

you are already whole.

Chapter 24 – The Merging of Observer and Life

All this while,
you have watched.

You became the witness—
the one who steps back,
the one who sees thoughts
as clouds across a vast sky.

You learned to notice
without clinging,
to allow
without drowning.

But now, something begins to shift.

The distance between 'you' and 'life'
starts to dissolve.
The observer is no longer

a separate figure,

standing apart.

The window through which you watched

becomes invisible—

and suddenly,

there is no watcher

and no watched.

Only watching.

This is the great merging.

Where breath is not *yours*,

it is simply breath.

Where thought is not an enemy,

but a passing ripple in the ocean.

Where life is not outside you,

nor inside you—

it is you.

The river flows,

and you are the river.

The bird sings,
and you are the song.
The breeze touches your skin,
and you are the breeze.

Nothing to observe.
Nothing to resist.
Nothing to protect.
Only presence—
pure, unbroken, infinite.

Here, the self that was striving to awaken
melts into the awakening itself.
The seeker disappears,
and only silence remains.

This is freedom.
This is union.
This is home.

A Quiet Moment for You

Close your eyes.

Do not try to observe.

Do not try to meditate.

Simply *be*.

Notice that life is already happening—

breathing, beating, flowing—

without your control.

Let go into that flow.

And recognize—

you and life were never two.

An Opening Into Presence

As you close this chapter, do not rush away.
Instead, pause for a breath—just one.
Notice the air entering, the air leaving, the quiet miracle that asks for nothing in return.

Allow yourself, even if only for a moment, to rest in this gentle awareness—
not as the thinker, not as the doer, but as the vast presence in which all things rise and fall.

In this pause, life is no longer separate from you.
It is you.

www.ingramcontent.com/pod-product-compliance
Ingram Content Group UK Ltd.
Pitfield, Milton Keynes, MK11 3LW, UK
UKHW021401190726
13845UKWH00028B/813

9 789334 402841